A People Gathered

Whales live in pods, geese gather in gaggles, lions form prides, bison move in herds, and human beings create communities. You know this already. You can name your communities—family, school, town, church, and so on. You know that human connections are deep, complicated, interesting, and sometimes frustrating.

The church knows that God has created us with a deep-down need to be with others. The church always seeks to gather us together. It all began when Jesus gathered the first small community of disciples around himself. That small assembly became a church that shared in Jesus' life. In the sharing each member grew closer to the others and closer to the Lord.

This course, *Gathering to Celebrate,* invites you to see the Catholic church as a people gathered around its Risen Lord. With prayer and great rejoicing, the church invites its members into the life of Christ through the sacraments of welcome—baptism, confirmation, and the Eucharist.

The church prays and rejoices in the forgiveness and healing sacraments of reconciliation and the anointing of the sick.

The church gathers to celebrate its members who commit themselves to the service of communion through the sacraments of marriage and holy orders.

This course can help you see how to become an active member of this gathering, celebrating people. It can help you deepen your life in Christ as you become a welcoming, healing, and serving person.

The Sacraments Defined

Sacraments are

_____

_____

_____

GOD'S
BELOVED
Sons and Daughters

In the desert the air crackled with excitement and anticipation as the people crowded around John the Baptizer. He announced the coming of the promised Messiah and offered a baptism of repentance. Many received this baptism and prepared to welcome the Messiah.

When Jesus left home to begin his lifework, he too went to John the Baptizer. He too stood among his people as one among many. He too was plunged into the waters of the river Jordan. But as Jesus came up out of the water, the sky opened. The Holy Spirit, soft as a dove, came upon him, and a voice echoed over the land: "Here is my beloved Son. In him I am well pleased."

On that day Jesus, a little-known carpenter of Nazareth in Galilee, was identified as God's beloved Son. On that day Jesus began the great work of his life.

From that day on, many people drew near Jesus and asked for healing and salvation. They sought to follow and stay with Jesus. A few disciples stayed with him throughout the brief years of his public life. They were gathered again with him after his death when he came to them as their Risen Lord.

Before Jesus returned to his Father in heaven, he passed on the gift that had been given to him—a share in God's life. Jesus blessed the Apostles and said: "All power on heaven and earth is given to me. Go now, and make disciples of all nations. Baptize them in the name of the Father and of the Son and of the Holy Spirit. And remember, I myself will be with you always, even to the end of all time." (Adapted from Mark 1:4–11; Matthew 28:18–20)

The Apostles did as Jesus commanded. Many people sought to become followers of Christ. They too wanted to be God's beloved sons and daughters. The Apostles

baptized these people with water. They placed their hands on the newly baptized, who then received the Holy Spirit. The Apostles invited these newly baptized and anointed people to share in the breaking of the bread.

The Sacraments Today

Today these actions of welcome and belonging are called the sacraments of initiation—baptism, confirmation, and the Eucharist. Special words and actions signify and make present the grace that is unique to each of these sacraments.

In baptism, water signifies death and life: Sin is washed away and new life in Christ is ours. Like Christ we are God's beloved sons and daughters. Like Jesus we can call God Father. We can call one another sisters and brothers.

Other signs are also part of the sacrament of baptism. The whole assembly gathers and promises to help the candidates live as good Catholics. The newly baptized persons are given a white garment as a symbol of their new life in Christ. They are given a candle as a symbol of their unity with Christ, who is our Light. Oil traced in the sign of the cross shows they are welcomed as God's beloved sons and daughters.

The celebration of the three sacraments of welcome has grown and changed over the past two thousand years or so, but new members of the church are still baptized with water, anointed with oil, empowered by the laying on of hands, and invited to share in the Eucharist. Today, however, the celebration of the sacrament of confirmation is often separate from that of baptism. Young people are confirmed during their teen years. At this time they receive the strength of the Holy Spirit through the laying on of hands. And they are again anointed, or blessed, with oil.

A Welcoming People

You belong to a people gathered by Jesus and called to share in his life. You are among the newest members of a worldwide church that has existed for about two thousand years. Like all members of the church, you live by the same faith. You share the same baptism, the same Communion, and the same mission to serve.

Your baptism began your life as a beloved son or daughter of God. This grace-filled life must continue in your attitude, words, and actions. How does your baptism show? How can you act as a loving, open, and welcoming son or daughter of God?

Life-Giving Words

In the early church, the word the first followers used to describe themselves was the Greek word *ekklesia.* This word means "a people whose members are summoned or called together." The word *ecclesial,* meaning "related to the church," is based on this Greek word.

Life-Giving Words

It is a great value for you to have faith.

. . . .

You are a chosen race,
a royal priesthood,
a holy nation.
You are a people of God's very own.
You can announce the mighty acts of God,
who has called you from darkness to wonderful light.
For once you were not a people,
but now you are God's own.
You who had not received God's mercy,
now have received it.

(Adapted from 1 Peter 2:7–10)

Our Unending Story

Narrator   Peter   James
Andrew   John

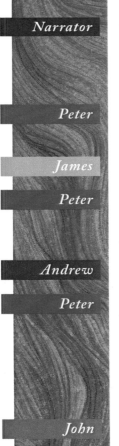

Narrator Two brothers, Peter and Andrew, are sitting under an olive tree. Another set of brothers, James and John, have just arrived. They have brought a few dried fish, some freshly picked figs, and a loaf of barley bread. They have dropped by to say good-bye to Peter, who is setting out for Rome in the morning.

Peter Well, tomorrow I leave for Rome. All my life I have lived here. I thought I'd be a fisherman—

James [excitedly] But you *are* a fisherman, Peter. A fisherman of people!

Peter I know, James, I know. I meant a catcher of plain, old, everyday fish. But then Jesus came walking along the shore and chose me and you, and you, John, and you too, Andrew.

Andrew Right. Me too. Can you believe it? Me.

Peter He spent three years with us, day and night. It took us a long time to understand all that he wanted to teach us. It took all the everyday things, like his opening his hands to everyone who came to him. Like his bending down to heal and comfort. Like his opening his arms to everyone—me, you, tax collectors like Zacchaeus, Pharisees who waited to argue with him, small children, all the people no one cared about.

John It's all true. He opened his arms to everyone.

Peter · The other day I was thinking about the night before he gave himself to his own death on a cross. It was Passover night, you know. Since I was a small child, every Passover meal had been exactly the same. We knew the story of our ancestors' freedom from slavery. We tasted the bitter herbs, we looked forward to the roasted lamb, we passed around the sweet wine and the unleavened bread. We thought we knew what to expect. But on that Passover night before Jesus died, he blessed and broke the bread and shared himself with us. He said he was the wine that was poured out.

Andrew We didn't understand that he was giving us his life as bread and wine. Jesus knew that one day we would understand.

John We have slowly understood that whenever we gather to break bread and remember all he told us, Jesus himself is with us. When we tell one another the stories, we remember what his presence is like.

Andrew All over Jerusalem now, small groups are gathering in homes to break bread and to remember and to pray together. The meal we shared the night before he died goes on and on and on.

Peter The stories are in our minds and hearts, that's for sure. I know the Lord is with us when we gather and celebrate his presence.

James | There's no telling where it will end. People could be breaking bread and sharing their lives together for a thousand years, Peter. A thousand years!

John | But tomorrow you have to begin your travel of hundreds of miles, Peter. It's time to get some sleep. The waters you will cross are greater than our little Sea of Galilee. The land, greater than our small country. Jerusalem looks tiny next to the imperial city of Rome. Your journey will be long, Peter.

Narrator | Peter journeyed to Rome and was a fisher of men and women and children, as Jesus said he would be. Peter is thought to have died there by crucifixion between the years 70 and 90. Tradition says that James and Andrew also died as martyrs. Only John lived to an old age.

The church in Jerusalem grew as the followers of Jesus devoted themselves to the teachings of the Apostles, to sharing their life together, to the breaking of the bread, and to prayer. Every day they faithfully and with full hearts met together in the area of the Temple, told the stories of Jesus, and shared bread in their homes. The community of believers was of one heart and one mind. No one among them was in need of anything. The Apostles gave witness to the Resurrection of Jesus, and great favor was given to all. (This last paragraph is based on Acts of the Apostles 2:42,46; 4:32–33.)

Our Unending Celebration

Liturgy of the Word

Introductory Rites

We gather in the name of the Father and of the Son and of the Holy Spirit.

Proclamation of the Word

We listen to readings from the Bible.

The first and second readings are from the Old Testament and from the Epistles, Acts of the Apostles, or Revelation in the New Testament. The first and second readings are read by lectors. One person who is a lector in our parish is

_____ .

The last reading is always from the Gospel of Matthew, Mark, Luke, or John. The Gospel is proclaimed and the homily is given by an ordained person—a bishop, a priest, or a deacon. In our parish the Gospel is proclaimed by

_____ .

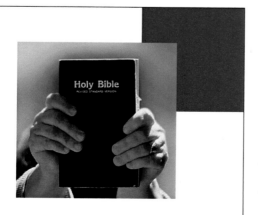

The Gospel story that has the most meaning for me right now in my life is

_____

_____

_____

_____ .

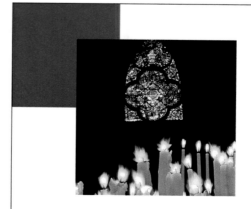

Liturgy of the Eucharist

Preparation of the Altar and the Gifts

We bring the gifts of bread and wine.

Eucharistic Prayer

The presider leads us in the eucharistic prayer, which speaks of our thankfulness and re-members and makes present the action of the Last Supper.

The Gospels of Matthew, Mark, and Luke all tell the story of the Last Supper. Though the three versions differ in small ways, they all tell of Jesus' action of taking, blessing, breaking, and giving the bread, which is his body. And they all tell of Jesus sharing the wine, which is his blood.

The Gospel of Matthew narrates the story of the Last Supper like this:

> While they were eating, Jesus took bread, said the blessing, broke it, and giving it to his disciples said, "Take and eat; this is my body." Then he took a cup, gave thanks, and gave it to them, saying, "Drink from it, all of you, for this is my blood of the covenant, which will be shed on behalf of many for the forgiveness of sins. I tell you, from now on I shall not drink this fruit of the vine until the day when I drink it with you new in the kingdom of my Father." (Matthew 26:26–29)

Communion Rite

The bread, which has been taken, blessed, and broken, is now given to us with the words, "The body of Christ." We say, "Amen," to express our faith in the true presence of Christ. We reverently receive the bread of Christ and return to our place in the assembly.

Dismissal Rite

At the end of the eucharistic celebration, the presider dismisses us with the formal command, "Go in peace to love and serve the Lord."

TO LOVE AND SERVE THE LORD

When you fully share in the eucharistic celebration, you are in communion with Christ and you are one in Christ with others. The dismissal rite commands you to go forth and *be* a eucharistic person—a person of peace and service.

Silently ask yourself these questions: What if the hungry world were not far away? What if the person in need were nearby? in my house? at school? in this room? How could I reach out and help?

Write your responses to these statements:

These are my best gifts and talents:

_____

_____

Someone I know seems to have this need:

_____

_____

I can share my best gifts and talents with the person I have in mind by doing this:

_____

_____

Life-Giving Words

Be doers of the word, not just listeners. For mere listeners just lie to themselves. They are like people who look in a mirror and see their face, then walk away and forget.

Do not be someone who hears and then forgets. Be someone who does and acts. Then you will be blessed. (Adapted from James 1:22–25)

Peace begins when the hungry are fed. (Anonymous)

Life-Giving Words

It is good enough to talk of God whilst we are sitting here after a nice breakfast and looking forward to a nicer luncheon, but how am I to talk of God to the millions who have to go without two meals a day? To them God can only appear as bread and butter. (Mohandas Gandhi)

MAKING IT Right

Read these cases, which require reconciliation, and pick the ones that you think are most valuable to talk about.

EXAMPLE

A friend and I steal a yield sign from an intersection in our neighborhood. My friend wants it for her bedroom.

CASE 1

I tell my mom off when Dad's not around. My mom doesn't say anything to me. She doesn't say anything to Dad either.

CASE 2

I tease my little brother until he cries and tells Dad. I tell Dad that my brother's always bugging me.

CASE 3

A kid in my class spread lies about me just before the school election for student body president. I lost by twenty votes.

CASE 4

I know this kid who has pornographic magazines. He lets me look at them any time I want.

CASE 5

Cheating in Mrs. McAllen's class is easy; she trusts us.

CASE 6

I usually dump most of my school lunch.

CASE 7

I tell Mom I'm going to the Saturday Mass, but I don't go.

CASE 8

When I'm mad at Dad for not giving me money, I just give him the silent treatment.

CASE 9

I get CDs from a kid who steals them and sells them for two dollars each.

Walking Together Again

Greeting

Proclaim It

LEADER. God's forgiveness is always first.

READER 1. May God open our heart and bring us peace. May we remember that God's mercy is always greater than our sins. When we are ready to take a small step, God is already waiting to take a thousand steps. When we are ready to walk toward God, God is already running toward us. When our sorrow is great, God's forgiveness is already overflowing. Let us begin in the name of the Father and of the Son and of the Holy Spirit.

ALL. Amen.

READER 1. Our reading is from the Gospel of Luke.

LEADER. [Read the Gospel story from Luke 15:11–24 or 19:1–10]

Examination of Conscience

Name It: Identify the Sin

LEADER. Let us recall together what troubles us inside, what puts a great distance between God and ourselves. Let us recall what puts a great distance between each of us and others. Let us place this difficulty before God.

READER 2. When our cutting words or long silences hurt . . .

ALL. God's forgiveness awaits us.

READER 2. For taking what is not ours, and for not taking care of what is ours . . .

ALL. God's forgiveness awaits us.

READER 2. For not respecting the health and well-being of our growing body . . .

ALL. God's forgiveness awaits us.

READER 2. For not being honest and fair . . .

ALL. God's forgiveness awaits us.

READER 2. For not bothering to pray alone or together with others . . .

ALL. God's forgiveness awaits us.

Claim It: Admit Responsibility for the Sin

READER 3. Now let us all pause for a moment of silence to decide the one area where we have failed to be God's beloved sons and daughters, and brothers and sisters to one another. *[All pause for reflection]*

Change It: Resolve to Improve and Make Things Better

READER 4. When we are ready, let us bring forward our footprint as a sign that we will take steps to stay with God, who comes to us with forgiveness. *[All bring forward their footprint and return with a candle and a scroll, as directed]*

Closing Rite

Proclaim It

LEADER. We are grateful for God's forgiveness, which allows us to forgive and ask forgiveness in return.

READER 5. When we are ready to take a small step . . .

ALL. God is already willing to take a thousand steps.

READER 5. When we are ready to walk toward God . . .

ALL. God is already running toward us.

READER 5. When our sorrow is great . . .

ALL. God's forgiveness is already overflowing.

READER 5. When we are ready to be brothers and sisters to one another . . .

ALL. God is already one with us.

READER 5. When we are ready to be God's sons and daughters . . .

ALL. God is already our Father.

READER 5. Let us all pray the words that Jesus taught us. Our Father . . . *[All join in the Lord's Prayer]*

LEADER. Let us now all depart in peace and gratitude, in the name of the Father and of the Son and of the Holy Spirit.

ALL. Amen.

Life-Giving Words

Put aside all that is false. Speak the truth to your neighbor. Be angry, but do not sin. Do not let the sun go down on your anger. . . . Be kind and filled with compassion for one another. Forgive, as God has forgiven you, in Christ. (Adapted from Ephesians 4:25–32)

Sins cannot be undone, only forgiven. (Igor Stravinsky)

Forgiveness is not an occasional act; it is a permanent attitude. (Martin Luther King Jr.)

The Sacrament of the Anointing of the Sick

DURING THE SACRAMENT OF ANOINTING, THE PRIEST SAYS TO ALL PRESENT:

My dear friends, we are gathered here in the name of our Lord Jesus Christ who is present among us. As the gospels relate, the sick came to him for healing; moreover, he loves us so much that he died for our sake. Through the apostle James, he has commanded us: "Are there any who are sick among you? Let them send for the priests of the Church, and let the priests pray over them, anointing them with oil in the name of the Lord; and the prayer of faith will save the sick persons, and the Lord will raise them up; and if they have committed any sins, their sins will be forgiven them."

Let us therefore commend our sick brother/sister [name] to the grace and power of Christ, that he may save him/her and raise him/her up.

THE PRIEST ANOINTS THE SICK PERSON'S HEAD AND HANDS AND SAYS:

Through this holy anointing
may the Lord in his love and mercy help you
with the grace of the Holy Spirit.
Response. Amen.

May the Lord who frees you from sin
save you and raise you up.
Response. Amen.

AFTER THE ANOINTING THE PRIEST SAYS:

Let us pray.
Lord Jesus Christ, our Redeemer,
by the grace of your Holy Spirit
cure the weakness of your servant [name].
Heal his/her sickness and forgive his/her sins;
expel all afflictions of mind and body;
mercifully restore him/her to full health,
and enable him/her to resume his/her former duties,
for you are Lord for ever and ever.
Response. Amen.

(The words of the sacrament of anointing on this page are quoted from
Pastoral Care of the Sick: Rites of Anointing and Viaticum.)

Love Without Measure

Unlike the woman in the rhyme who had so many children she didn't know what to do, Clara McBride Hale had many, many children, and she knew *exactly* what to do.

Long, long ago Clara's husband died, when their children were only five and six years old. Clara did not want to leave them to work in other people's homes, so she began taking care of children in her home. Over the years she took care of forty children.

Clara retired when she was sixty-four years old. For a brief while, there were no children in her home in Harlem. Then one day Clara's daughter sent a girl with a crack baby to her. What was Clara to do? She took the baby in.

Then social workers brought another, and another, and another. Within two months Clara was caring for twenty-two babies. The social workers thought *they* were bringing the crack babies to Clara's door, but she knew better. "[God] kept sending them, and . . . kept opening a way for me to make it," she said.

Clara had a magic way with babies, but this magic is available to everyone. She held the babies and rocked them in her old, used rocking chair. She told them they were beautiful and great and good. By and by everyone called Clara "Mother Hale," and Clara's home became "Hale House."

Hale House bulged with children, and new space was found. And new babies came—AIDS babies. Unlike crack babies, the AIDS babies would not become healthy again. Their life would be very short, and Mother Hale would just have to pour all the life and love she had into the little time they had. "I want them to live a good life while they can and know someone loves them," she said.

Over the years old Mother Hale took in more than six hundred addicted or infected babies. She rocked them to sleep and told them how beautiful they were until one day in December 1992, when God called her home to tell her how beautiful she was. God must have told her face-to-face, and Mother Hale must have smiled.

Life-Giving Words

O God, that we may receive your blessing, touch our brows, touch our heads, and do not look upon us in anger.
In a hard year, offer us mercy; in a year of affliction, offer us kindness;
dark spirits banish from us, bright spirits bring close to us;
gray spirits put away from us, good spirits draw near us.
When we are afraid, offer us courage;
When we are ashamed, be our true face;
be over us like a blanket, be under us like a bed of furs. Amen.

(Mongolian)

A Personal Prescription

"Whatever you did for anyone, even for the one others considered of little importance, you did for me." (Adapted from Matthew 25:40)

Write a prescription that you can fill for someone's well-being. Begin following this prescription as soon as possible!

_____

_____

_____

_____

_____

No Greater Love

The twelve friends Jesus chose to be his Apostles stayed with him for all three years of his public ministry. On the night before he died, one Apostle, Judas, left the company of friends and betrayed Jesus.

Jesus told the eleven who stayed with him: "I give you this great command, that you love one another. No one has greater love than this, than that he lay down his life for his friends. You are not my servants, for servants do not usually know what their master is doing or thinking. I call you friends, for I have told you everything that the Father has told me."

That night, all the Apostles except John abandoned Jesus. John and Mary, Jesus' mother, stood by him on the day he was crucified. Mary Magdalene and another friend named Mary were also there with Jesus.

On the evening of the first Easter Sunday, the Risen Jesus came to his Apostles, who were hiding because they were afraid and confused. Jesus kept his commitment to the friends he had chosen. He reached out to them and offered them his peace.

(This recounting is based on John 13:21–30; 15:12–15; 19:25–26; 20:19–21.)

Promises to Keep

According to the Gospel of John, Jesus' first miracle took place at a wedding in Cana, near his hometown. In this story Jesus turned water into wine because he did not want the newlyweds to be embarrassed. They were running out of wine, and there were many people at the wedding. The story ends with the words "Jesus did this as the beginning of his signs in Cana in Galilee and so revealed his glory, and his disciples began to believe in him" (John 2:11).

Today this story helps us believe that the union of a bride and groom is a sign of the union of Christ with us. The abundance of good wine at Cana points to the abundance of God's blessings on the couple, and on all of us.

Jesus' respect for the strength and durability of marriage continued among his followers and is present in the church today. In the sacrament of marriage, or matrimony, the vows exchanged by the bride and groom are the primary signs of the sacrament. The closing blessing of the Marriage Rite helps us understand the newlyweds' commitment to the larger community in which they will live as husband and wife.

Life-Giving Words

Happy are you who honor the Lord
and walk in God's ways.
You will enjoy the work of your hands;
your work will prosper;
your wife will be a fruitful vine
and your children will sprout up
around your table.
This is how the blessed ones
honor the Lord.
May the Lord bless you
all your life.
May you share Jerusalem's joy.
May you live to see your children's children.
May peace reign in Israel!

(Adapted from Psalm 128)

The Exchange of Vows

Before a man and woman exchange their wedding vows, they declare that the covenant they are about to make is freely undertaken, is lifelong, and is open to the procreation of children.

Then the man and woman are ready to exchange wedding vows. They say:

I, [name], take you, [name], to be my wife [or husband]. I promise to be true to you in good times and in bad, in sickness and in health. I will love you and honor you all the days of my life.

The husband and wife also exchange rings:

[Name], take this ring as a sign of my love and fidelity. In the name of the Father, and of the Son, and of the Holy Spirit.

The Closing Blessing

At the end of the wedding, the presider blesses the couple by saying:

May your children bring you happiness, and may your generous love for them be returned
to you, many times over.

. . . .

May you have true friends
to stand by you. . . .
May you be ready and
willing to help and
comfort all who come to
you in need.

. . . .

May you find happiness . . . in your work.

. . . .

May the Lord bless you with many happy years together, so that you may enjoy the rewards of a good life.
And after you have served [the Lord] loyally . . . on earth, may [the Lord] welcome you to [the] eternal kingdom in heaven.

(The words of the sacrament of marriage on this page are quoted from *Rite of Marriage*.)

Life-Giving Words

Love is all we have, the only way / that each can help the other. (Euripides)

When you love you wish to do things for. You wish to sacrifice for. You wish to serve. (Ernest Hemingway)

The love we give away is the only love we keep. (Elbert Hubbard)

A Lifelong Commitment

The wedding day marks the beginning of a lifelong loving commitment between a husband and wife.

To Lead Is to Serve

...Act 1...

Narrator. Before the feast of Passover, Jesus knew he would soon leave this world and return to his Father. He loved the friends he would leave behind to carry on his work. He loved them to the end.

During the feast he rose from the table and tied a towel around his waist. He poured water into a basin and began to wash the Apostles' feet.

Peter. *[horrified]* Are you going to wash my feet?

Jesus. I know you do not understand now, Peter, but you will understand later.

Peter. *[protesting]* Oh, no. You will never wash my feet.

Jesus. *[softly but firmly]* Well, Peter, unless you let me do this, you will not share in my life.

Peter. *[with new enthusiasm]* In that case wash my feet. And wash my hands and head as well!

Narrator. So Jesus washed Peter's feet, and he washed all the Apostles' feet. Then he returned to his place at the table.

Jesus. Do you know what I have done? You call me master and teacher, and you are right to do so. But if I am your master and teacher, then learn from my example. I have done the work of servants. You too should do the work of servants if you are to follow me. I tell you solemnly, when you welcome even the smallest one who comes to you, know that you are welcoming me.

(This act is based on John 13:1–20.)

Act 2

Narrator. The disciples carried on the mission of Jesus. They preached the good news of Jesus as the Risen Lord. Those who joined the Apostles were of one mind and heart. As more and more people joined the followers of Jesus, trouble arose.

New followers. We do not speak the language of your people. We only speak Greek. So none of you understand the needs of our people. We have widows and orphans who are being neglected. They go away cold and hungry.

Apostles. We cannot proclaim the Good News and take care of everyone's needs too. We need to appoint seven good and holy men to care for the needy.

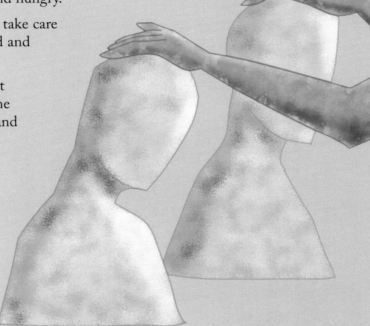

Narrator. The whole assembly agreed. They brought before the Apostles Stephen, Philip, and five others. The Apostles placed their hands on the heads of the seven and appointed them deacons.

(This act is based on Acts of the Apostles 6:1–6.)

Epilogue

Writings about the early church referred to its leaders as bishops and presbyters and deacons. The word *bishop* means "overseer." The bishop's vocation was to oversee the activities of the local church. His vocation was to keep all the baptized in the communion of the one faith proclaimed by the Apostles. As time passed the local church grew to be called the diocese, a collection of parish churches in a given area.

Presbyters served in local communities that gathered to break bread, to proclaim the Gospel, and to care for those in need. Again as time passed, the presbyters were called priests, and the smaller communities were called parishes. Deacons served in ministries of caring for the poor and needy.

A clear pattern of leadership in the church—deacon, priest, and bishop—grew as the church grew. This pattern of leadership also linked the local churches to one another and linked the church to the Apostles.

THE FIRST DAY

The day of ordination is the first day of the life of a young man who becomes a priest. On that day the bishop speaks for himself and for all the people present when he says,

> We rely on the help of the Lord God and our Savior Jesus Christ, and we choose this man, our brother, for priesthood in the presbyteral order. *(The Rites of the Catholic Church as Revised by Decree of the Second Vatican Ecumenical Council and Published by Authority of Pope Paul VI,* volume 2, page 61)

To show their agreement that this man is worthy and ready to become a priest, the people respond,

> Thanks be to God. (Page 61)

The bishop silently lays his hands on each man to be ordained. Afterward he extends his hands and prays:

> Almighty Father,
> grant to this servant of yours
> the dignity of the priesthood.
> Renew within him the Spirit of holiness.
> As a co-worker with the order of bishops
> may he be faithful to the ministry
> that he receives from you, Lord God,
> and be to others a model of right conduct.
>   (Pages 66–67)

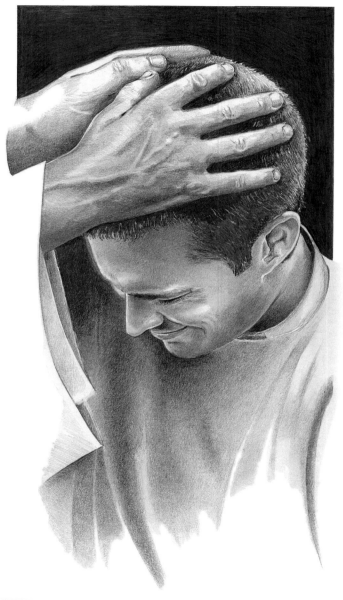

The bishop anoints the hands of the new priests with oil. He then gives each priest a stole and chasuble and a chalice and paten as symbols of his ministry.

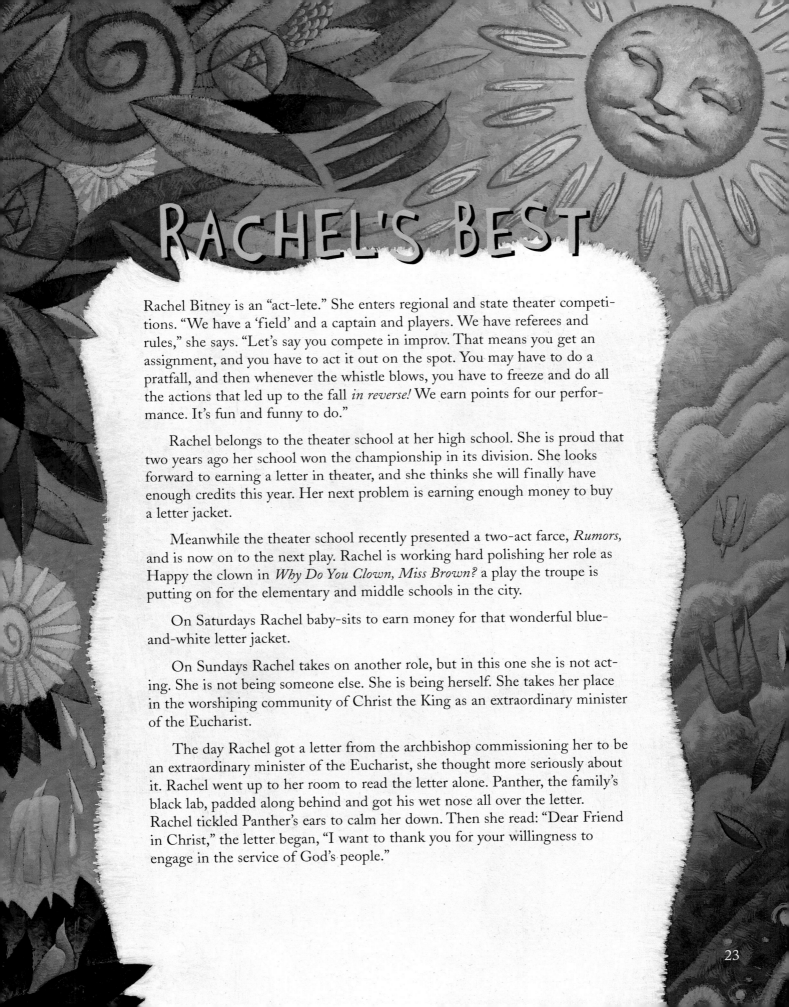

RACHEL'S BEST

Rachel Bitney is an "act-lete." She enters regional and state theater competitions. "We have a 'field' and a captain and players. We have referees and rules," she says. "Let's say you compete in improv. That means you get an assignment, and you have to act it out on the spot. You may have to do a pratfall, and then whenever the whistle blows, you have to freeze and do all the actions that led up to the fall *in reverse!* We earn points for our performance. It's fun and funny to do."

Rachel belongs to the theater school at her high school. She is proud that two years ago her school won the championship in its division. She looks forward to earning a letter in theater, and she thinks she will finally have enough credits this year. Her next problem is earning enough money to buy a letter jacket.

Meanwhile the theater school recently presented a two-act farce, *Rumors,* and is now on to the next play. Rachel is working hard polishing her role as Happy the clown in *Why Do You Clown, Miss Brown?* a play the troupe is putting on for the elementary and middle schools in the city.

On Saturdays Rachel baby-sits to earn money for that wonderful blue-and-white letter jacket.

On Sundays Rachel takes on another role, but in this one she is not acting. She is not being someone else. She is being herself. She takes her place in the worshiping community of Christ the King as an extraordinary minister of the Eucharist.

The day Rachel got a letter from the archbishop commissioning her to be an extraordinary minister of the Eucharist, she thought more seriously about it. Rachel went up to her room to read the letter alone. Panther, the family's black lab, padded along behind and got his wet nose all over the letter. Rachel tickled Panther's ears to calm her down. Then she read: "Dear Friend in Christ," the letter began, "I want to thank you for your willingness to engage in the service of God's people."

The archbishop's letter also contained a booklet about the Eucharist and eucharistic ministers. Rachel tried to read the booklet, but she didn't understand a lot of it. She felt honored to be chosen. "I think it shows that I care enough about my religion," she says. "I feel proud when I stand next to the priest. I feel like a soldier, like I am standing for something."

So on Sundays Rachel Bitney takes her place at the head of the long line of friends and family and fellow worshipers. "Even if I do this a million times, it's different from acting. It's me. It is like working, not like presenting a play. I remember this when I see kids I haven't seen since we were in junior high. Even the kids who are goof-offs are serious when they come forward to receive Communion. They don't act silly, you know? Communion is something we grew up with. It feels like it has been part of us all our lives. Now I get to give the whole parish the body and blood of Christ."

Life-Giving Words

A *Prayer* FOR THOSE WHO *Serve*

O God:
Enlarge my heart, that it may be big enough to
    receive the greatness of your love.
Stretch my heart, that it may take into it all those
    who, with me, around the world, believe in
    Jesus Christ.
Stretch it, that it may take into it all those who
    do not know him, but who are my
    responsibility because I know him.
And stretch it, that it may take in all those who
    are not lovely in my eyes, and whose hands
    I do not want to touch; through Jesus Christ,
    my Savior. Amen.

(African)